...ut that birthday cake. How I cried when the sky let go with a cold and lonesome rain.

Mamma smiled, said "Don't be sad, child. Grandma's watching you today."

heaven,

er tears ar   down.

're lonely just remember she can see,

there's holes in the floor of heaven and she's watching over you and me.

ching, wishing

she could be here now.

his sleepy little town. I thought we'd grow old together. Lord, I sure do miss her now.

ou're lonely

just remember she can see.

e her lovely smile.

ning down, she takes my hand, says "Daddy don't be sad 'cause I know Mamma's watching now."

s watching over you and me.

For

_____

From

_____

Date

_____

I dedicate this book

with much love and admiration

to my grandmother,

Florence Dean Glover,

and my dear friend Kenny Craft.

I miss you terribly.

— Steve Wariner

HOLES
IN THE
FLOOR
OF
Heaven

STEVE WARINER

I AM A FIRM BELIEVER IN FATE AND DESTINY. I TRULY FEEL THE GOOD LORD MAKES EVERYTHING HAPPEN FOR A PARTICULAR REASON.

The morning Billy Kirsch and I got together and wrote this song, my "brilliant" words were: "Hey, let's write something that's rockin' and up-tempo!" My wonderful wife/publisher Caryn overheard our conversation from the kitchen and reminded us we had never written a story song together—one that really tugged at the heartstrings. At that point Billy said, "Hey don't laugh at me but I think  I've got an idea. My wife Julie overheard someone say this phrase: '…there's holes in the floor of heaven.'" Well, I just about fell over! Thanks Billy, and thank God for those wives!

I've been so fortunate over the years to have had several hits and number ones, but I've never had a song with an overwhelming response like "Holes in the Floor of Heaven." Everyone has someone in life whom they love but have lost. This song speaks directly about that loss but does so in a positive, uplifting way.

The letters, stories, and e-mails I've received have been absolutely incredible. The following pages are great examples that I felt compelled to share with you. I hope they touch you in the same way they touched me and will remind you to take advantage of every second you have to let the ones you love know exactly what's in your heart while they're still here with you.

I dedicate "Holes in the Floor of Heaven" to all our loved ones we have lost from this life who wait for us on the other side. Very gratefully and humbly, I thank those who contributed to this book of letters and those who helped bring this song into being. May each of you find a glimpse of heaven as you read these stories and peek through the open cracks in the clouds of eternity.

Humbly yours,

Steve Wariner

HOLES
IN THE
FLOOR
OF
Heaven

by Billy Kirsch & Steve Wariner

One day shy of eight years old

When Grandma passed away,

I was a brokenhearted little boy

Blowing out that birthday cake.

How I cried when the sky let go

With a cold and lonesome rain.

Mamma smiled, said "Don't be sad, child.

Grandma's watching you today."

'Cause there's holes in the floor of heaven

And her tears are pouring down.

That's how you know she's watching,

Wishing she could be here now.

And sometimes if you're lonely

Just remember she can see;

There's holes in the floor of heaven and she's

Watching over you and me.

Seasons come and seasons go;

Nothing stays the same.

I grew up, fell in love,

Met a girl who took my name.

Year by year we made a life in this sleepy little town.

I thought we'd grow old together.

Lord, I sure do miss her now.

But there's holes in the floor of heaven

And her tears are pouring down.

That's how I know she's watching,

Wishing she could be here now.

And sometimes when I'm lonely

I remember she can see.

There's holes in the floor of heaven and she's

Watching over you and me.

Well, my little girl is twenty-three,

I walk her down the aisle.

It's a shame her mom can't be here now

To see her lovely smile.

They throw the rice, I catch her eye

As the rain starts coming down.

She takes my hand, says "Daddy don't be sad

'Cause I know Mamma's watching now."

And there's holes in the floor of heaven,

And her tears are pouring down.

That's how you know she's watching,

Wishing she could be here now.

And sometimes when you're lonely

Just remember she can see.

There's holes in the floor of heaven and she's

Watching over you and me.

He heals the brokenhearted

and binds up their wounds.

— Psalm 147:3

Now you just remember this—
heaven is as blissful and lovely as it can be;
but it's just the busiest place
you ever heard of.

— Mark Twain
"Captain Stormfield's Visit to Heaven"

DEAR MR. WARINER:

I wanted to write and let you know how your song has touched my family.

My mother and son, Jared, were real pals —he brightened her life and when she was lonely she would call and have him stay with her. When he was mad at us, he would go next door to Grandma's house.

In April, my mom had a stroke and gradually went downhill. Jared and I were watching a country music show and heard "Holes in the Floor of Heaven." Jared started singing along, and I was already crying when he said, "Mom, if something happens to Grandma, I want them to play this song."

We did play it at her funeral in November. I was up front, and Jared was sitting behind me where I couldn't see him. Everyone was sobbing—except for Jared. My brother told me Jared was smiling with a very contented look on his face and no tears. He will be nine years old in January, and his grandma won't be here for the first time, but I'm sure we'll play the song for her that night.

— Kim Albert

Holes in the Floor of Heaven　　　　13

Talk to God as you would

talk to your very best friend.

Tell The Holy One everything.

— Rebbe Nachman of Breslov

Blessed be the LORD,

because He has

heard the voice

of my supplications!

—Psalm 28:6

I COME FROM A VERY CLOSE FAMILY. In the late night hours one September, my mother called to give me the sad news that her older brother Bob had just passed away of a heart attack. Her younger brother Jim was told of Bob's death the next day, which was also Jim's forty-ninth birthday. We were all in shock, but Jim was having a very hard time with it. In March we were all still trying to deal with the loss when Jim unexpectedly passed away. Because of the two deaths being so close, it hit everyone in the family twice as hard.

I went back to work the next night. The first song played on the radio station we listen to was "Holes in the Floor of Heaven." When I heard it, I couldn't move and had to fight back the tears.

We laid my Uncle Jim to rest on April the second. My mother was coming to pick me up for the funeral when she heard the song for the first time on her car radio. She experienced the same feeling that I had when I first heard it at work. After we left the funeral home, we heard the song on the radio again as we drove to the cemetery. We both believe it sounds like my uncles are talking to us through you and your song. Thank you again for a wonderful and very heartfelt song.

—Peggy Beam

Holes in the Floor of Heaven

I thank you so very much for your song "Holes in the Floor of Heaven." My husband passed away suddenly one January. He left behind two girls, Michelle, who was eight years old, and Ashley, who was four. I had told our girls, "Daddy has gone to a beautiful place with God, and we will see him again." That didn't seem to help them until we heard your song. Now every time it is on the radio we turn it up. We sing along, and it gets us through and it makes them smile — more so on rainy days. They are so very happy to know Daddy watches over them. I know God gave you a wonderful talent to help others.

God bless you and your family,
Elizabeth Beatty

Let the peace of God

rule in your hearts.

—Colossians 3:15

You've touched my heart with your song! My Grandma Becky was a very active, goofy, lovable seventy-year-old. She loved dancing, country music, and a new "love" named Walter! She was expected to make a full recovery from Hodgkin's disease, but developed viral pneumonia and gradually lost the ability to even respond to us by nodding her head. She died the day before my twenty-sixth birthday.

When we took a trip to Nashville, my husband and I visited The Grand Ole Opry and heard you perform "Holes in the Floor of Heaven." Tears rolled down my face. It was as if you were speaking specifically to me. They weren't tears of sorrow, but tears of joy! I felt as if Grandma Becky were there looking down upon us. Thank you for such a memorable event and a heartfelt song.

— Tracy Blue

No matter what you are thinking now,
where there's future…there's hope.

—Kenny Rogers

Trust in Him
at all times, you people;
Pour out your heart before Him;
God is a refuge for us.

—Psalm 62:8

I AM A MOTHER OF TWO BOYS: BRYAN IS FIVE AND JOHN IS THREE. A couple of months ago their father had an accident at work and passed away. It was one of the hardest things I've had to go through. One day we were in the car and your song came on the radio. I was already in tears when my five-year-old asked, "When it rains does that mean Daddy's watching over us?"

It's so hard trying to make two small boys understand why their daddy died, but every night I pray and every day the boys and I listen to "Holes in the Floor of Heaven" and that makes us believe everything will be okay, somehow, some way.

—Lisa Brescia

W hen my master reaches down,
I'll be there.
Takes me to that higher ground,
I'll be there.
I felt lonely, lost, and hollow,
He gave me roads that I could follow.
When my master reaches down
I'll be there.

—Spiritual

I don't usually write fan mail— this is not a fan letter either. This is a thank you letter. My mother passed away one July, and if it hadn't been for your song, I would've taken her death a lot harder. The song is very special to me and my family. Your song was played at my mother's funeral, and it started raining about the same time.

I also believe in fate... as you say you did on the cover of the album, and that one day I'll be reunited with both my mother & father.

Thank you & God bless!

Darlene Brown

Today is the door
into forever
when we
believe.

I BELIEVE THINGS HAPPEN FOR A REASON, AND I HAVE FAITH THAT GOD KNOWS EXACTLY WHAT HE'S DOING. I truly believe this song was released at a time meant just for me! My childhood was about as perfect as anyone could ask for. I was a happy child until my mom was in a fatal automobile accident when she was only thirty-seven years old. I was thirteen then. This event changed my whole life. There hasn't been a day that goes by that I don't think of her. There have been times in my life when the emptiness of her absence was especially painful—such as on my wedding day.

I'm thirty-one now and, after a miscarriage last year, my husband and I are expecting our first child in six weeks. It's a very exciting time of life for us and even though I feel blessed by God to be experiencing this miracle, I also find myself longing for my mother's presence. "Holes in the Floor of Heaven" reminded me that she's with me every day, and it gave me the best feeling to think she's watching over me and has been ever since her death.

My mother always loved the rain, so the rain has always been special to me.

—Lisa M. Collins

Holes in the Floor of Heaven

HEATHER STAYED WITH HER GRANDFATHER AND ME UNTIL SHE TURNED SIXTEEN, AND LIVED WITH HER FATHER. She wanted to be a social worker to help problem children. God is taking care of her, but our hearts are still broken. Enclosed is a poem one of Heather's friends wrote the night she died. God gave her the strength to write this!

Heather was my very good friend;
    We never thought it all could end.
She will always be in my prayer;
    Even though my heart feels bare.
We all really miss her so
    And look to heaven to see her glow.
Every time it rains and pours,
    I wonder if she watches from the holes in its floors.
I know everyone is in sorrow and pain,
    But God always has a plan with something to gain.
I grew to love and cherish her as a friend,
    And I know in my heart I will be with her in the end.

—Cortney Danielle Hoevener

Words don't mean much at a time like this, but writing my thoughts about Heather helps me to deal with all of this. I know in my heart that she would want us to move on, because she was so excited about graduation. She'll always be with us in our hearts and minds, though now she's somewhere much more divine. I love and miss her so, and I'll never forget her.

—Marie Lee

Holes in the Floor of Heaven

STEVE, YOUR SONG IS FOREVER ENGRAVED IN MY MIND AS "CHERRI'S SONG." Cherri is my very precious daughter, who died as a result of a vehicle accident . She was twenty-six years old.

The very first time I heard your song was on our return trip from Oklahoma City to Colorado the day after my daughter died. It tore at my heartstrings, because as the song began, small raindrops started to fall on the windshield of our truck. They seemed to last just the length of the song. We swore that Cherri was watching and traveling home with us.

Cherri's death was very tragic, and we all feel her tremendous loss. She was going to a town on the other side of Oklahoma City to pick up her two children, Chase, who was three, and Megan, just twenty-two months old.

I requested that your song be played at her services, but the musicians couldn't get the background music. But after the service, when we had all gotten into our vehicles for the drive to the cemetery, your song started to play on the radio. My husband and I both shed tears and knew that Cherri was with us. After we had all gathered at the cemetery I had more than one person approach me with the same thought, for they had heard your song also. As the service was about to conclude, small drops of rain started to fall. It was never hard, just very light. Your song entered my mind, and I had to lift my eyes up to smile at my daughter— for she was sending her love to us all.

—Paula K. Lindsey

Surely goodness and mercy
shall follow me all the days of my life;
and I will dwell in
the house of the LORD forever.

—Psalm 23:6

The Bible promises God's people that we will one day see those we miss again.

That hope causes us to look toward heaven in expectation of wonderful reunions to come.

Holes in the Floor of Heaven

29

*...and a little child
shall lead them.*

—Isaiah 11:6

WHEN I FIRST HEARD YOU SING "HOLES IN THE FLOOR OF HEAVEN," IT OPENED UP A FLOODGATE OF CHILDHOOD MEMORIES. I am a seventy-eight-year-old grandmother, but when I was seven years old my baby sister, who was two years old, died rather suddenly. Of course, I was consoled by my parents and grandparents, who told me she'd gone to heaven to be with Jesus and the angels.

A few nights after her funeral, I was on the front porch one night gazing into the dark sky when I noticed how millions of stars were constantly twinkling. Then I knew for sure there were holes in heaven and she and the angels were walking along over them, which caused the twinkling. This was a great comfort to me, and I readily accepted the fact that she was surely in the presence of angels.

—Alma B. Mallory

Dear Steve,

My name is Sarah Lowe and I am 7½ and I like your songs, but I really like Holes in the Floor of Heaven because I think of my Grandmom.

Love,

Sarah Lowe

How excellent
the heaven,
When earth
cannot be had;
How hospitable,
then, the face
Of our old neighbor,
God!

—Emily Dickinson
1830–1886

I RECENTLY LOST THE ONLY GRANDMOTHER I'D EVER KNOWN DUE TO A CAR CRASH JUST A FEW MILES FROM HER HOME. We were very close because we both have a love for music. She loved to hear me play and sing. She also loved you [Steve] as an artist, but especially the way you play guitar. Of all the songs that were on the radio at the time, my grandma had honestly told me that "Holes in the Floor of Heaven" was her favorite. It went to number one on the charts the day she died and has kept me going in the last few weeks. There's not another song anywhere that means more to me.

I was her only grandchild, and at her funeral I requested the song to be played. I couldn't help but cry and smile at the same time when the song began because I truly knew that there are holes in the floor of heaven. After the funeral, I had to go and get ready for my high school graduation the same night. Just a few days before she died, grandma said she wanted to go to my high school graduation because she would never make it to see my college graduation.

She was there because of "Holes in the Floor of Heaven."

—Jason McFarland

Faith is not the belief that God will deliver what we want when we want it, but that He has gracious control of our lives and that He will be faithful to direct our paths and give us the grace to walk through life's unpredictable times.

—Bernadette Keaggy

I HAD A GRANDDAUGHTER, CHANIE RANEE, WHO WAS FOUR-AND-A-HALF YEARS OLD. SHE PASSED AWAY IN JANUARY. To begin with, she knew you [Steve] when she saw you on the television. We always watched the Country Music Channel, and when she would see you she would say, "There's Steve, Mawmaw." She also knew the words to some of your songs, and she would sing along with you. Not too long after she passed away, your song "Holes in the Floor of Heaven" came out, and I felt like this was her going-away song from one of her favorite people.

My heart has been broken many times in my fifty-three years, but this time the mending will be painfully slow. Keep up the good work. I know Chanie can hear all your songs in heaven.

—Patsy Sims

In March I lost my nineteen-year-old son, Marc, in a head-on collision. Three years ago I would have expected a call from someone telling me something had happened to him because of his personal battles, but not this year. Through persistence, a lot of love, and support from family, friends, and colleagues, he won those battles, was finally growing up, and had found his niche in life as a competitive ballroom dancer and instructor. Marc wanted to give back to others in gratitude to those who had helped him, so he decided to continue a program at a new studio for children and young adults to learn how to dance and participate in competitions and thus feel good about themselves. The morning after his most successful night as a professional, he and his partner were hit head-on by a stolen vehicle. Marc was killed instantly.

It didn't make sense—just when his life was finally on a positive track. We're not supposed to bury our children or grandchildren. That next morning my mom and I both woke up at the same time hearing a miracle and blessing of the most beautiful song: "Holes in the Floor of Heaven." We cried after hearing it, but we also felt as if everything would be fine. Somehow we knew Marc was now safe and happy. My only explanation to this tragedy is that God must have needed Marc to help teach the angels to dance!

—Ruth L. Tucker

Now I saw in my dream that by this time the pilgrims were got over the Enchanted Ground, and entering into the country of Beulah, whose air was very sweet and pleasant. . . . Yea, here they heard continually the singing of birds, and saw every day the flowers appear in the earth. In this country the sun shineth night and day. . . .

—John Bunyan
The Pilgrim's Progress

Holes in the Floor of Heaven

I LOVE CHILDREN AND SEEING THEM SMILE GIVES ME THE GREATEST FEELING. I'd sit and play with my friend Rachel's little daughters, Shaila and Shelby, for hours. One day we got the news that Shelby, age three, had passed away. I heard your song while looking at Shelby's picture, and I didn't feel sad that she was gone because I could picture her looking down on all of us from the holes in the floor of heaven.

That beautiful three-year-old, whose smile I loved and whose hugs I treasured— I knew she was smiling down. I wasn't so much sad that we'd lost her, but happy because I knew she was laughing again and being the same gorgeous little girl for everyone in heaven that she had been for all of us here on earth.

I'd been so depressed about losing Shelby, but your song reminded me that she's in a beautiful place now and she's still making everyone's lives happier and giving us all a reason to smile.

—Chris Wilcher

FIVE DAYS BEFORE MY TWENTIETH BIRTHDAY, THE MOST BEAUTIFUL WOMAN IN THE WORLD FINISHED HER JOURNEY ON EARTH AND BEGAN HER WALK WITH JESUS. I only wish I could live the Word of God as strong as she did.

The night my grandma passed away from cancer, I talked to Jesus and began to realize the finality and nearness of death and began to see your song for what it is. It's got to be one of the most beautiful songs ever written. It talks of many hard times, but shows that we must go on and believe in God to stay strong. As I listened to your song, it began to mirror my life.

In years past I used to frown on rain because it meant I had to stay inside or couldn't play baseball or soccer. Now, after hearing your song, I love to hear the sound of rain on the rooftop.

—Joshua Wright

THIS SONG MEANS SO MUCH TO MY DAUGHTER, HEATHER, AND ME. It came
at the perfect time. Heather was pregnant with her first child, and she was told
that the baby wouldn't make it because it had no kidneys or bladder. She went
full term and had Michael-Marie on June twenty-third. My beautiful granddaughter lived for only one hour,
but we loved her so much. She died
in my arms. Whenever we play your
song—which is a lot—we sing and
smile, knowing you taught us that
there truly are holes in the floor of
heaven. We know that she watches
over us, and I look forward to the rain
now. You put such feeling into that song, and it goes right to our hearts. Thank you.

We wonder what she would look like and what kind of person she would
have grown up to be, but you make it a little easier, knowing that she can see us
and be assured that we are always thinking about her. We love you for that.

—Shirley Edwards

When I hear your song come on television or radio, I quit whatever I am doing & listen. I lost my daughter, Shirley, in 1984, lost my husband in 1988, & lost my son in 1988. So you can see why that song about "Holes in the Floor of Heaven" will always have a place in my heart. I love them all so much, & I get lonesome for them.

Dovie Franklin.

I FELT LIKE THROWING STONES AT A SILENT SKY WHEN I FOUND OUT MY MOTHER HAD CANCER. People might have reproved and admonished me had I told them my feelings. But God didn't. Instead, in His time, He touched and healed my angry, hurting spirit.

—Joy Jacobs

I ALWAYS THOUGHT THAT A GIRL'S SIXTEENTH BIRTHDAY WAS SUPPOSED TO BE HER BEST, BUT MINE WAS THE WORST IN MY LIFE BECAUSE I WAS TRYING TO COPE WITH THE LOSS OF MY GREAT-GRANDMA. She meant everything in the world to me. She always took care of me. It was the hardest thing I've ever had to deal with.

Your song really helped me out a lot. I know she's watching over me. I wanted to write and let you know you're an inspiration. I hope you keep continuing what you do, and I wanted to say "Thanks a lot."

—Hope Fugate

Holes in the Floor of Heaven

N ever despair! Never!
It is forbidden to give up hope.

—Rebbe Nachman of Breslov

YOUR SONG IS MY FAMILY'S STORY. My mom and dad had four kids, and in April Mom was diagnosed with brain cancer after being found in a coma one morning. Just this last November, my grandmother passed away, and in January my mom went to be with the Lord at age forty-six. We miss her a lot. Because of your song, I think of her each time it rains.

My sister Emily is getting married to her hometown sweetheart, Keith, in July. We all wish my mom could be here to see it, and we know she'd be here if she could.

—David Gabel

Love cannot be acquired but only given.
The love you give is the love you have.
And the more people you love,
the more love you have.

—Lawrence Kushner

THE FIRST TIME I HEARD YOUR SONG I CRIED LIKE A BABY BECAUSE ALL I COULD THINK OF WAS MY MOM! When I lost her I felt like I had lost my right arm! I really felt like a part of me died inside, like part of me went to the grave with her. She was my best friend, and so it makes this birthday just a bit sad and lonely without her here to share it with me. That's why your song means so much to me, because I imagine her looking down and being with me in a special way!

—Nancy Frye

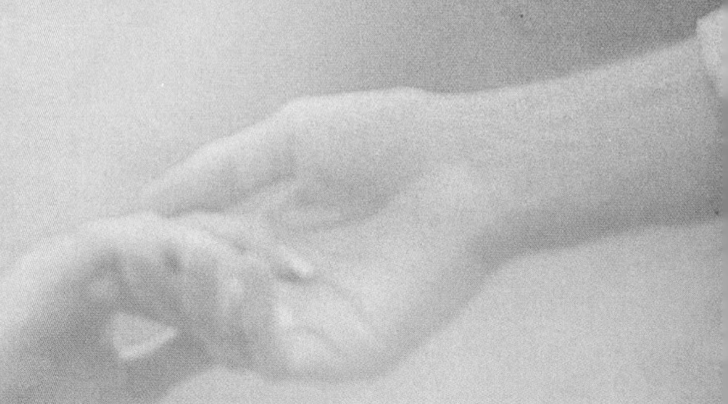

Going to Heaven!

I don't know when—

Pray do not ask me how! . . .

If you should get there first

Save just a little space for me

Close to the two I lost—

The smallest "Robe" will fit me

And just a bit of "Crown"—

For you know we do not mind our dress

When we are going home.

— Emily Dickinson
1830–1886

For we know that if our earthly house,

this tent, is destroyed,

we have a building from God,

a house not made with hands,

eternal in the heavens.

—2 Corinthians 5:1

My father passed away seven years ago next month, and my mother passed away two years ago last June. In that time I started a practice of putting seasonal flower arrangements on their graves throughout the year and balloons for their birthdays, anniversary, and Mother's and Father's Days. I would guess that at least ninety percent of the time when I would change the flowers or put on a balloon, it would start to rain. A lot of the time it wouldn't look like rain while I was driving to the cemetery. One day after leaving the cemetery soaking wet from the sudden raindrops, your song came on the car radio, and I finally realized why it would always rain when I was at my parents' grave. I believe there are holes in the floor of heaven and Mom and Dad are crying happy tears for the flowers and balloons we bring for them and for the wonderful memories.

—Janice L. Alexander Ginn

FOR FIVE SHORT YEARS I WAS MARRIED TO MY BEAUTIFUL WIFE. I met Linda at the Payette County Sheriff's Office where she was a patrol deputy and I was a jailer. We started dating in September and were married in November. It was your typical whirlwind romance. We bought a house and began to add to our family. I was promoted to patrol deputy and Linda was soon promoted to patrol sergeant—so she became my boss at work as well as at home!

We were at the highest point in our lives when I was awakened one night by our doorbell ringing. I opened the door and there stood my captain, Willie, and my sergeant, Greg. I knew instantly something was wrong. Captain Willie said, "Chad, Linda has been shot and killed." I will never forget those words as long as I live.

Linda was raised on a large ranch in Oregon. She loved horses, was very athletic, and had scholarships to many colleges for volleyball, basketball, and rodeo. My life has changed forever, and I'm just now starting to sleep again. Our children, Clinton, Rena, and Zachary are doing well, and I am truly blessed to have such a wonderful family and so many wonderful friends.

—Charles Huff

I s not God in the
height of heaven?
And see the highest stars,
how lofty they are!

—Job 22:12

One of the things that makes us

look toward heaven as our home

is knowing that

the people who have made

our earthly houses into our homes

will be waiting for us there.

MY GRANDMA WAS A "SPUNKY" LITTLE LADY. She never complained the whole time she had cancer, which was about eight to ten years. She was a loving lady and Sundays were always set aside to be at Grandma's . It was a tradition! So thanks for such a lovely song—it keeps her memory alive!

—Donna Helms

Whom have I in heaven but You?

And there is none upon earth

that I desire besides You.

— Psalm 73:25

I AM PLANNING TO GET MARRIED, AND I'M MAKING SURE WE HAVE AN INDOOR WEDDING. I know it will rain, because my grandpa in heaven will be thinking of me. His love will never be lost as long as I have my memories.

I grew up with my "Papa" and would spend every weekend with him and my grandma. We had a great time together, but one January he had a stroke and refused to go to the hospital. Over the phone I talked him into going and came to drive him there. He had to be put in a nursing home and thought he would never see his house again. He almost gave up hope. With his family by his side, he relearned all the things he used to do.

That summer my grandparents celebrated their fiftieth wedding anniversary. We gave them a huge party at their home, and I've never seen my grandpa have so much fun. It was great to see my Papa do so well after his long struggle.

On December eighteenth I said good-bye to him, gave him a kiss, and told him that I would see him when I got back from my dad's. He had another stroke and left so fast that no one got to say good-bye. I'd never felt so empty, so heartbroken—I had lost a great person who meant the world to me. A couple of months after his death I heard your song and fell in love with it right then and there. Because of your song, I know my Papa is safe—and someday I will see him again.

—Jamie L. Hovet

The hills and
valleys of heaven
will be to those
you now experience
not as a copy
is to an original,
nor as a substitute
is to the genuine article,
but as the flower
to the root,
or the diamond
to the coal.

—C. S. Lewis

Holes in the Floor of Heaven

PLEASE DON'T RUSH LIFE. Take time and relax. Hug and kiss your children and let them know you love them. Life is very short. I've learned that the hard way. I play your song for my son who passed away of Sudden Infant Death Syndrome. He was only a month old. Your song really helps me when I'm down and sad. Every day I say thanks to God for my two-year-old son. Children are so precious.

—Crystal L. Hurd

God calls our loved ones,
    but we lose not wholly
What He has given;
They live on earth
    in thought and deed
      as truly
As in His heaven.

—*John Greenleaf Whittier*
1807–1892

Holes in the Floor of Heaven

I KNOW IT'LL BE HARD FOR EVERYONE, BUT I'M USING "HOLES IN THE FLOOR OF HEAVEN" TO DANCE WITH MY FATHER ON MY WEDDING DAY THIS JUNE. It's just too perfect—I have to use it! I just hope by then I'll be able to listen to the whole song without crying, but I probably won't.

A friend of mine told me about the song, and when I heard it, that was the first time I cried for my mother in front of anyone.

It'll be two years since my mother passed away. She suffered for one year and eight months before she died of ovarian cancer at only fifty-five years of age. It's been very hard for me, although I don't let it show. I'm the youngest of five children, and I feel like I need my mom the most, especially now. My fiancé, Trevor, and I truly believe that my mom got us together. I only wish she were here now to see me so happy and so in love.

—Jennifer N. Jacino

You hold me by my right hand.

You will guide me with

Your counsel,

And afterward receive

me to glory.

— Psalm 73:23–24

I LOVED MY GRANDMOTHER WHEN I WAS EIGHT YEARS OLD AND STILL DO BECAUSE SHE WAS MY HEART. Before she passed away, she told me that there is never just one answer to a question. She would always hold me in her arms while she read in her chair. She was an Indian woman who was very wise. But there was one bit of wisdom I could never forget. On her deathbed she said she wanted me to be in her arms, because she had one last thing to tell me. She said every time it rained, she was thinking of me.

As the years passed and it rained, just like today, I would sit outside in the rain alone and think of her — but especially today. This my sixteenth birthday, and I thank Mr. Wariner for his song. Now I can look at a picture of Grandmother without crying. I miss her dearly, but I've learned how to let go.

—Amanda Jump

Once in a dream I saw the flowers
That bud and bloom in Paradise;
More fair are they than waking eyes
Have seen in all this world of ours.

—*Christina Rossetti* (1830–1894)

One day shy of eight years old when Grandma passed away, I was a brokenhearted little boy

And there's holes in the floor

'Cause there's holes in the floor of heaven and her tears are pouring down.

That's how you know she's watching, wishing she could be here now

And somet

That's how you know

she's

Seasons come and seasons go; nothing stays the same. I grew up, fell in love, met a girl who took

Year by year we mad

And sometimes whe

Well, my little girl is twenty-three, I walk her down the aisle. It's a shame her mom can't be he

They throw the rice, I catch her eye as the

There's holes in

the floor of heaven and